how to

LEAD A
PERSON TO
CHRIST

I believe the vast majority of Christians have a great desire to lead people to Christ, but many are not quite sure how to go about it. If this is your situation then this booklet is just for you.

We know of course salvation is a work of the Holy Spirit and people are not won to Christ by human argument or by simply praying a prayer but by a true work of the Holy Spirit, which brings conviction of Sin, Repentance and a deep desire to follow Jesus. But the Bible says "and how shall they believe in Him of whom they have not heard?"

Romans 10:14)

As we declare the Great Gospel Message people are convicted of their sin and come to Christ.

Just a few days ago I was telling the story of Jesus to a middle aged lady and she started to cry and was really moved in her heart and I had the privilege of leading her to Jesus, the truth of the Gospel just touched her.

Reasons Why We Share Our Faith

Commissioned by His Word

Then Jesus came to them and said, All authority in heaven and on earth has been given to me. Therefore go and make disciples of all Nations, baptising them in the name of the Father and of the Son and of the Holy Spirit.

Matthew 28:18-19

Jesus has given us authority to preach the Gospel - <u>to tell His story</u>. We all have different personalities and characters, which is wonderful, and are all part of God's plan to win the lost. You will be able to relate to some people that I cannot and vice versa. Some are quiet violins, some loud trumpets, that's all right.

Be yourself but be sensitive to the people and the Holy Spirit's guidance. Jesus gives us His commission and strength through His Word, the Bible.

Motivated By His Love

For God so loved the world that He gave His one and only Son, that whoever believes in Him shall not perish but have eternal life.

John 3:16

If we only tell about Jesus out of legalism and without a genuine concern for others we will not be very effective in winning people to Christ.

I remember a story I heard many years ago about a lady who married twice. Her first husband was very strict and would order his wife about, he even wrote out a set of rules for her, e.g. how she should arrange the furniture, what to cook and many other things. She did all these things dutifully.

This man eventually died. Years later the lady remarried. The second husband was so different from the first. He did all he could to help her and with his kindness he made her very happy. One day the lady found the set of rules her first husband had made her follow, she looked at the rules and to her surprise she found she did all the same things for the second husband as she had done for the first. The difference was she was now doing it out of love and not because she was made to.

The apostle Paul said, for Christ's love compels us.

2 Corinthians 5:14

Our passion for Jesus gives us a deep compassion for people.

Empowered By His Spirit

But you will receive power when the Holy Spirit comes on you; and you will be my witnesses in Jerusalem, and in all Judea and Samaria, and to the ends of the earth.

Acts 1:8

We have the person of the Holy Spirit living within us. Without Christ we can do nothing, people are not won to Christ by human argument but by the working of the Holy Spirit.

The Holy Spirit will direct and guide us as we witness, as we stay close to the Lord Jesus in the way that we live.

An elderly gentleman was cleaning the Church where he worshipped. He was a lovely Christian, but he was not well this particular day as he set about to vacuum the carpets. He worked for about an hour because the area was quite large.

He didn't realise until the end of the hour that the vacuum cleaner was not plugged in and the whole time had been wasted.

We are sometimes like this in our Christian lives - we do not plug into the power source.

"Make sure to plug into the source."

Co-workers with God

For we are God's fellow workers; you are God's field, God's building.

1 Corinthians 3:9

1 Corinthians 3:7-9 encourages me so much.

It is not my responsibility to save the lost but it is my responsibility to tell His story, the rest I leave to Him.

People turn to Christ through the work of the Holy Spirit as they come to genuine repentance and desire to follow Jesus.

We just need to live close to Jesus and allow Him to work through us. It is exciting working alongside Jesus, because people are always challenged to change.

"The Gospel is the power of God unto salvation."

Reasons We Do Not Share Our Faith

Sometimes we need to overcome obstacles to sharing our faith. I've just listed a few that sometimes stop us, so that we can overcome them.

1) Fear - This is a major struggle for some. Remember our Lord Jesus makes us all different; some of us are quiet and some are Loud, but God uses our different personalities. If we are quiet or noisy He can still use us to win people to Him. Allow Him to help you and pray and ask God to help you to overcome this obstacle and if you need to, ask your Pastor or Church leader to pray for you.

2) Guilt - The Bible says the devil is the accuser of the Brethren, he will be quick to point out our mistakes. Maybe we have problems at home, perhaps a partner or children are unsaved. Don't be deterred but remember the precious blood of Jesus cleanses all sin.

3) Inadequacy - Most of us feel inadequate occasionally. It is at these times especially that we need to know the source of our strength. People are won to Christ not through self-effort but through the conviction of the Holy Spirit. Our strength comes from Christ so we can boldly go and tell His story.

4) Lack of knowledge - I am amazed that sometimes people do not realise the seriousness of the Gospel, that without Christ people go to Hell. Let us never lose the urgency of preaching the Gospel.

5) Lethargy - This is simply being self-centred instead of Christ centred. Let us pray for God to help us when we don't feel like sharing our faith.

6) Too busy - Sometimes we need to evaluate the way we spend our time. To win people to Christ we need to not only meet unsaved people but spend time with them. Some times we are very busy attending meetings but not so good at putting the message into action.

7) Departmentalisation - Beware of limiting evangelism to those on the "Evangelism Team" only, as the Lord wants us all to have the joy of sharing this great message.

8) Lack of success - Sometimes we set unrealistic goals and become discouraged when these are not reached. It is not our responsibility to save but Christ's.
Our responsibility is simply to share Jesus every day in a way that people can understand.

LIST HERE SOME THINGS WHICH WOULD PREVENT YOU FROM SHARING YOUR FAITH:

....

....

....

....

....

....

....

Let's pray right now and ask our Lord Jesus to help us overcome them.

"Dear Lord Jesus,
You know how I love you so much and want to win people for you. But so often many things hold me back. I surrender my life afresh to you and ask you to liberate me to overcome every obstacle and share my faith."

People are God's Priority

When Jesus saw the people He had compassion for them. Because they were like sheep without a shepherd.

Matthew 9:36

It is when we see the people our hearts are touched because we know without Christ there is no hope for forgiveness, cleansing, freedom of guilt or heaven. Jesus loves people all types of people, young, old, black, white, educated, uneducated, rich, poor, religious, non-religious. God's great love touches our heart, and Jesus gives us compassion for the people.

Our Personal Preparation

The greatest preparation we have is to walk close to Jesus.

1) We need to know Christ as our personal Saviour.
2) Be filled with His Holy Spirit.
3) Have a prayerful attitude.
4) Earnestly desire to not only read the Bible, but by our lifestyle show Jesus.
5) Develop our prayer life, prayer and evangelism really do go together. We are the temples of the Holy Spirit, 1 Corinthians 6:19 and the Holy Spirit in us will guide us to people and people to us who are searching for Christ.

Getting Ready

Your True Story

Learn to share your own personal story (testimony) off by heart in 2-3 minutes.

You'll be absolutely amazed at the power of your personal story - people love stories particularly true ones!

Never underestimate the effect of your story.

And they overcame him (Satan) by the blood of the Lamb and by the word of their testimony.

Revelation 12:11

Sharing your testimony will lift you up, and encourage you, as you tell others what God has done for you!

Next time you feel a bit down, try telling someone your testimony, you'll be amazed at how it will lift your faith and calm your fears. When the chips were down for David - he encouraged himself in the Lord I Samuel 30:6.

Your testimony will also encourage others that they too can experience what God has done for you.

Let's look at some examples from the bible of the Dynamics of Personal Testimony.

Example 1

Read John 4:1-42

Many of the Samaritans from that town believed in Him because of the woman's testimony.

John 4:39

This account of Jesus talking with the women at the well gives us some wonderful facts, her name is not recorded, but we do know that she was a divorcee five times over, hallelujah - God is a God of the second chance!

The woman went immediately to tell her story to her town and what fantastic results it had! Many Samaritans from the town believed because of her story.

Example 2

Read Mark 5:1-20

What did Jesus say to the man in verse 19?

....

....

....

....

....

....

What was the result of his testimony?

....

....

....

....

....

....

....

The account says he went away and began to tell in The Decapolis, how much Jesus had done for him (verse 20).

The Decapolis was ten cities, so the man travelled to ten cities telling his story of how Jesus had delivered him from many demons, and if you follow through in the Gospels you will see that he actually became the `forerunner' of Jesus in these towns, where many believed because of the one man's story!

Example 3

Read John 9:1-34

The thing we can learn from this account is that you don't have to be a great theologian or Bible scholar to be mightily used of God. Look at the answer the man gives to the Pharisees who were asking him to tell them who had performed the miracle and how it had happened.

He replied, "Whether he is a sinner or not, I don't know - one thing I do know I was blind but now I see!"

it was as simple as that!

That's the lovely thing about these three accounts - they are ordinary people, not scholars or theologians.

One was divorced five times over!
One was so demon possessed that the demons walked and talked through him!
And one was blind from birth and didn't know anything about anything!

Some Guidelines on Giving Your Testimony

Write your story without using any 'churchy,' religious words. It will help you and the listener if you split your story into sections for example.

a) Before I became a Christian (this should be concise and honest, but not too gory!)

....

....

....

....

....

b) How I became a Christian (Why, When, Where, How!)

....

....

....

....

....

c) Since I became a Christian (go to town here telling what great things God has done for you.)

....

....

....

....

....

Emphasise on (c) since I became a Christian.

I remember asking two young people to share their story in an evangelistic meeting. The one, a young girt who came to Christ when she was 3 years old, the other a young man who had come to Christ following a term of imprisonment. The young girt said to me "I've no story to give because I've always been conscious of Jesus since a baby because I've been brought up in a Christian home".

I said to the young lady, "You've got a wonderful powerful Testimony took what the Lord Jesus has saved you from".

We've all got powerful testimonies when we've walked with Christ. Because we are different, every story is unique so it's not mass produced but wonderfully different to the Glory of God.

Prayer of Commitment

Learn a sinner's prayer. This will be a guideline you can use with people who are coming to Christ.

I usually pray something like this.

> Dear Lord Jesus,
>
> I believe you are the Son of God and died on the cross for me. I am really sorry for all the bad things I have done in my life. Please forgive me and clean my life up. I turn to you Lord Jesus and turn away from these wrong actions and I ask you to come into my life, help me to follow you and please make me a true Christian.
>
> Thank you.

Write out your own sinner's prayer and learn it off by heart, so that you are ready to bring someone to Christ as you share your faith.

....

....

....

....

....

....

Know The Message

The Bible tells us

- There is one true God
- Jesus is the Son of God
- He died a sacrificial death for our sins
- He rose from the dead and is alive today
- He offers forgiveness, cleansing and freedom of guilt
- There is a heaven to gain
- A hell to turn away from
- We can come to know God personally.

Gospel Presentation

God Loves People

"For God so loved the world that He gave His one and only Son, that whoever believes in him shall not perish but have eternal life."

John 3:16

People's Problem

We have gone our own way and not God's, turned our back on Him, and become self-centred.

For all have sinned and fall short of the glory of God.

Romans 3:23

Result of Sin/Separation

For the wages of sin is death, but the gift of God is eternal life in Christ Jesus our Lord.

Romans 6:23

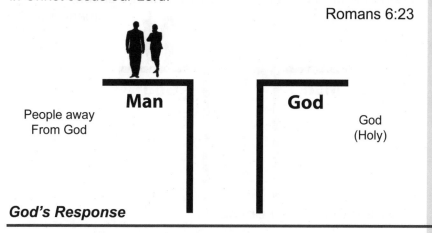

People away From God

Man

God

God (Holy)

God's Response

But God demonstrates His own love for us in this, while we were still sinners, Christ died for us.

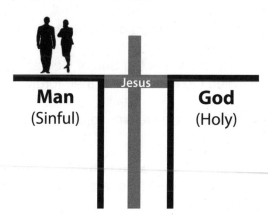

Jesus

Man (Sinful)

God (Holy)

People's Choice

That if you confess with your mouth "Jesus is Lord" and believe in your heart that God raised Him from the dead, you will be saved.

Romans 10:9

For it is with the heart that you believe and are justified, and it is with your mouth that you confess and are saved.

Romans 10:10

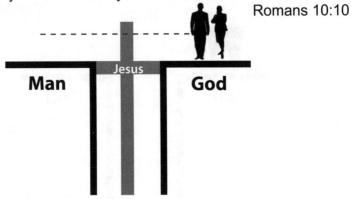

A Person Coming To Christ

Needs to: -

Admit   They have sinned and turned from God

Believe   That Jesus is the Son of God and that He died On the cross for their forgiveness.

Confess   That they have sinned and turn to Christ.

When you share the Gospel emphasise a need for Repentance, Forgiveness, Hope and the Lordship of Christ. Acts 3:19

Presenting the Good News

Some guidelines to help you:

- Rely on the Holy Spirit to guide you, remember more can be accomplished in a moment by the Holy Spirit's work than a lifetime of self-effort
- Keep the presentation basic, aim to communicate not baffle the person
- Establish a rappore
- Speak clearly
- Don't use religious language
- Be approachable, don't be too intense/friendly
- Try not to baffle the person with lots of Bible verses but do use the Bible as your authority.
- Be open to the Holy Spirit as you are talking
- Quietly pray in your heart
- Learn to share your own personal story in a few minutes
- Learn a sinners prayer of commitment
- Be a good listener
- Be open to the Spiritual Gifts
- Don't be put off by awkward questions
- Admit if you don't know the answer
- Never lose your temper (don't argue)
- Be wise if speaking to children, make sure other people are around
- Ask God for divine appointments
- Know the materials you are using
- Carry a small Bible, Gospel literature
- Always leave the person in a manner so that someone else can speak to them.

Leading a Person to Christ

Leading a person to Christ is one of the greatest joys in life!

I think the most difficult part of sharing our faith is starting a conversation.

Practice Some Conversation Starters

e.g. If I meet a lady with children I start chatting about the children and ask how old they are etc.

e.g. If I meet a young person I ask what courses they are studying in college etc.

(I even talk about the weather)

It it is important to smile, have eye contact and be relaxed as you speak to make the person you are speaking to feel comfortable.

- Try to establish a rappore

- Don't forget to smile

- Do be a good listener

- Talk to them on their level

The survey in this booklet is a great tool. It is a great conversation starter and leads directly into giving your Testimony, Gospel message and challenge to come to Christ. We have used this survey in "one to one" witness for many years all over the U.K. Wherever we have used it we have never had less than 41 out of 50 people say yes to the last Question - "If you could know God personally would you be interested Yes/No?"

I am not saying 41 out 50 come to Christ, but I am saying more people are open to God than we ever realise.

For the person you will meet regularly and long term you can be slower in your approach. Christians with a passion for God just invite conversation when they are in long term situations.

If you are meeting someone once in a lifetime you can share the Gospel effectively in a few minutes if needed.

Survey

1. Do you believe in God?   Yes/No

2. Who do you think Jesus Christ is?

a. A Good Man
b. A Prophet
c. The Son of God
d. A Myth or Legend

3. What do you think happens when you die?

a. Re-incarnated
b. Nothing
c. Go to Heaven/Hell

4. If you could ask God one question, what would it be?

a. Why don't you reveal yourself to people?
b. Who created God?
c. Why is there so much pain and suffering in the world?
d. Something else

5. If you could know God personally would you be interested?

Yes/No

Guidelines

To Lead a Person to Christ

- Establish a rappore

- Share your true story

- Present the Gospel

- Challenge the person to come to Christ (e.g. after hearing all this would you be prepared to give your life to Jesus and follow Him?)

- If they say yes. Pray the sinner's prayer of commitment with them and have them to repeat it out loud, or they may prefer to pray their own prayer.

- Do not say to them you will have to wait to come to Church or see the Pastor. Pray with them there and then and lead them to Christ.

- Pray with them and ask God to bless them.

- Answer any questions they may have.

- Arrange for them to be followed up if possible.

Effective Follow Up

I am sure you will be thrilled to bits to have led the person to Christ, what a privilege.

Encourage the Person you have led to Christ

- To buy a Bible and read from the Gospels first (I always encourage them to read from Mark's Gospel because it's the shortest and full of the wonderful miracles of Jesus).

- To pray to the Lord using this simple acrostic;
  J - Jesus - Thank Him
  O - Others - Pray for others
  Y - Yourself - Pray for yourself

- Attend a Bible Believing Church.
- Tell another person about your new found faith in Christ.

If you live locally perhaps it will be possible for you to take them to Church with you or for you to direct them to a church.

If possible to swap contact details so that you can keep in touch, that would be good. (But be careful with people of the opposite sex). In that case it's better to give the church contact details.

Remember these are the nuts and bolts of leading someone to Christ, but only Jesus, by the person of the Holy Spirit can save a person.

Praise the Lord, He wants to use you!

Praying for People

Make a list of people you are praying for and aiming to present the Good News to.

....

....

....

....

....

....

....

....

....

....

Prayer and Evangelism, go Hand in Hand.

My prayer is that this little booklet will encourage you that God can and wants to use you to win the lost.

"Dear Lord Jesus,

I pray with all my heart that the reader of this little booklet will win many people for Christ. I pray that the anointing power of the Holy Spirit comes upon them in a special way to share their faith.

Thank you precious Lord of the Harvest in Jesus Name. Yes!"

Other Books By Marilyn Harry

● Changing Spiritual Atmospheres

● Equip

Courses Available

● Harvest Time School of World Evangelism

● Harvest Time Summer School of Evangelism

● Evangelism Training Days

For further information of Harvest Time Ministries with Evangelist Marilyn Harry (including 'Love Wales'):

E mail: harvest-time2000@hotmail.com
Web Site: www.harvest-time.org.uk

E mail: lovewales@live.com
Web Site: www.lovewales.org

Telephone: 01633 856783